COUNTRIES OF THE WORLD

CHINA

CARLOE GODDARD

Facts On File, Inc.

TITLES IN THE COUNTRIES OF THE WORLD SERIES:
AUSTRALIA • BRAZIL • CHINA • EGYPT • FRANCE • GERMANY • ITALY
JAPAN • KENYA • MEXICO • UNITED KINGDOM • UNITED STATES

China

Facts On File, Inc.
132 West 31st Street
New York NY 10001

Library of Congress Cataloging-in-Publication Data
Goddard, Carole.
China / Carole Goddard.
p. cm. — (Countries of the world)
First published: London: Evans Brothers, c2004.
Includes bibliographical references and index.
Contents: Introducing China—Landscape and climate—Economic development—Population—Transport and trade—Environmental challenges.
ISBN 0-8160-5506-8 (hc)
1. China—Juvenile literature. I. Title. II. Countries of the world (Facts On File, Inc.)

DS706.G63 2004
951—dc22 2004047097

Printed in China by Imago

10 9 8 7 6 5 4 3 2 1

Endpapers (front): A spectacular view of the Great Wall of China.
Title page: Four children pose in front of a rapeseed field.
Imprint and Contents pages: The dramatic landscape of Guilin.
Endpapers (back): The skyline of Hong Kong.

Editor: Katie Orchard
Designer: Jane Hawkins
Map artwork: Peter Bull
Charts and graphs: Encompass Graphics, Ltd.

Photograph acknowledgments:
front cover top, 13, 33, 36, 41, 43, 46, 47, 50, 53, 55 (Mark Henley); front cover upper middle and lower middle, front endpapers, 6–7, 28, 42, 58, 60, 61, back endpapers (Corbis Digital Stock); front cover bottom, 5, 15, 30 (Edward Parker); 8 (Nick Bonetti, Eye Ubiquitous); 9, 12, 14, 17, 19, 21, 37, 45, 56 (Popperfoto/Reuters); 10, 29, 32, 34, 35, 40, 48, 49 (Nigel Hicks); 11 (Geoff Daniels, Eye Ubiquitous); 16, 25, 54 (Fritz Hoffman, Document China); 18 (Wang Gang Feng, Panos Pictures); 20, 39 bottom (Alain Le Garsmeur, Panos Pictures); 22 (Robert Francis, Hutchison Library); 23, 26, 51, 57 (Julia Waterlow, Eye Ubiquitous); 24 (Dermot Tatlow, Panos Pictures); 27, 39 top (Chris Stowers, Panos Pictures); 31 (Sarah Errington, Hutchison Library); 44 (Melanie Friend, Hutchison Library); 52 (Associated Press).

First published by Evans Brothers Limited,
2A Portman Mansions, Chiltern Street, London W1U 6NR, United Kingdom.

The Chinese flag has a red background with five stars on it. The large star represents the Communist Party. The other four stars represent soldiers, farmers, workers and students.

The spectacular Great Wall is the national symbol of China.

China is a vast, ancient country, which today is changing rapidly as it becomes part of the modern world. The only countries with a greater area than China are Canada and Russia. In terms of population, however, China is the word's largest country, with 1.3 billion people, or 22 percent of the world's population.

China has one of the world's oldest and greatest civilizations, dating back about 7,000 years. The valleys of the Yellow and Yangtze Rivers were home to early cultural centers. A philosopher named Confucius (531–479 B.C.) had a strong influence on Chinese values, especially regarding the importance of the

family. But it was the first emperor, Qin, who unified China's people between 221 B.C. and 206 B.C. He introduced a new administrative system, strengthened the army and ordered the first Great Wall to be built. He standardized China's written language, legal code and currency.

Chinese culture, goods, and inventions (which include gunpowder, printing and paper) have spread across the world. From about 200 B.C. to A.D. 1500, the Silk Road led westward from Xi'an, linking China with the Mediterranean region. Caravans traveled along the Silk Road, carrying commodities from China to Europe, including silk, porcelain and jade. Today, Chinese people, as well as goods, have spread across the globe. All major cities across the world have a Chinatown district, and almost all towns have a Chinese restaurant or take-out.

People in Beijing take to the streets to celebrate the news that the city has been chosen to host the 2008 Olympics.

Communist China

On 1 October 1949, the leader of the Chinese Communist Party, Chairman Mao Zedong, announced the formation of the People's Republic of China. This marked the beginning of a new era in Chinese life. Under communist rule, China's development has been mapped out in a series of Five Year Plans. For 30 years all planning was strictly controlled by the central government, but in 1979 a new leader, Deng Xiaoping, introduced new policies to transform the economy.

Deng's Changes

In just over 20 years dramatic changes have spread across much of eastern China. Changes in agriculture, industry, science and technology, as well as improved contact with foreign countries, have all contributed to the success of Deng's plans. The growth of industry and a movement of people from the countryside to the cities have meant a new way of life for many Chinese people.

After Deng Xiaoping became the country's leader, China's economy grew at a rate of about 10 percent a year – faster than any other less economically developed country (LEDC). Increasingly China is playing a role on the world stage. The country joined the World Trade Organization in 2001, and in May 2003, the new president, Hu Jintao, attended the Evian G8 summit, a meeting of the world's most powerful leaders.

KEY DATA

Official Name:	People's Republic of China
Area:	9.6 million km^2 (mainland China)
Population:	1.3 billion
Official language:	Mandarin Chinese
Main Cities:	Beijing (capital), Shanghai, Chongqing, Chengdu, Harbin, Tianjin, Wuhan, Qingdao, Guangzhou
GDP Per Capita*	US$4,329
Currency:	Yuan
Exchange Rate:	US$1 = 7.4 yuan £1 = 13.6 yuan

* Calculated on Purchasing Power Parity basis
Source: World Bank

The spectacular first bend on the Yangtze at Shigu near Lijiang.

China has an amazing range of major landforms, rivers, climates and types of vegetation. Each physical region has a distinct climate and vegetation, often giving it a very different character from other parts of the country.

High Landscapes

Plateaux and high mountains make up almost two-thirds of China; in the west, the Qinghai-Tibetan Plateau covers over a quarter of the country. Its average height is 4,000m but from its lake-studded surface mountain chains rise to more than 6,000m. China has seven of the world's twelve peaks over 8,000m. Along the Qinghai-Tibetan Plateau's northern edge lie the Kunlun mountains. Along its southern edge are the Himalayas, forming the boundary between China and Nepal. The highest peak is Mount Everest at 8,849m. The high mountain peaks are snow-covered all year round; frost action and the many glaciers have sculpted dramatic scenery in the high mountains. High mountains also occupy much of eastern China. Their slopes have been deeply carved by the many rivers flowing down them.

Lowlands and Deserts

Only about a quarter of China's landscape lies below a height of 500m. The North China Plain, mainly less than 100m high, is the largest area of lowland in the country. The plain was formed by silt deposits laid down by the Yellow River.

China's only other low-lying plains are found along the middle and lower course of the Yangtze River and in the much smaller Pearl River Delta.

The northwestern regions of China are home to its desert areas, which make up over 20 percent of the country's total land area. The largest sandy desert in China is the Taklimakan. The Silk Road runs along its northern and southern edges. Severe sandstorms disoriented travelers on the Silk Road and many of them died on the journey.

LANDSCAPE FEATURES

RIVERS

China has many rivers, but the Yangtze and the Yellow River are by far the most important. They rise in the Qinghai-Tibetan Plateau and flow in a generally easterly direction.

The Yangtze is China's longest river at 6,380km. Its descent from the plateau is steep, and rapids mark its course as it flows at great speed through a series of deep, narrow gorges. At the eastern end of the famous Three Gorges region, the Yangtze leaves the mountains behind. It becomes a very wide river and flows in a series of bends, or meanders, over flat plains. Its vast delta extends from Nanjing to the East China Sea.

The Yellow River is China's second longest, at 5,464km. It flows through deep gorges in its upper reaches. Then for part of its middle course it flows in an enormous bend through the Loess Plateau, picking up huge amounts of loess on its journey. It is the world's most silt-laden river, carrying about 1.6 billion tonnes of silt per year. In parts of its lower reaches the Yellow River has built up its bed 10m above the surrounding plain. Levees (embankments) line this 700km stretch of the river's course across the North China Plain. The Yellow River flows into the Bo Hai Sea, but during severe floods, the river has changed its course to the sea several times. Such floods have resulted in devastating loss of life caused by drowning and starvation where the floods damaged crops. For this reason the Yellow River is also known as China's Sorrow.

A camel train crosses the vast sand dunes in Gansu Province.

EASTERN CHINA: A MONSOON CLIMATE

The weather plays an important role in the lives of Chinese people. Farmers are especially dependent on the weather, because crops may fail if they do not get the sunshine and rainfall they need. But the weather is important in cities, too: In Shanghai weather agents now advise businesses when to stock up on weather-related items such as umbrellas and turn on air conditioning.

Eastern China experiences a monsoon climate. In winter the land cools more quickly than the sea. Cold, dry winds blow out from the central area, bringing very low temperatures to the north and, in spring, clouds of dust to northern cities. South of the Qinling Mountains, which act as a barrier to these cold winds, the winters are milder, especially in the extreme south.

Most of China gets about three-quarters of its rain during the summer, from mid-June to mid-September. Southeasterly winds blow in from the sea, bringing heavy rain to the southeast coast, though not every day is wet. But the monsoon rain is variable, and drought and floods are hazards. Southeast China is very wet, but rainfall decreases northward and inland, and northwest China is arid.

Summers are unpleasantly hot and humid in both the north and south. During hot weather (30°C and over), air pollution in Beijing rises and hospitals fill with patients suffering from respiratory diseases such as asthma. Some people feel that such weather conditions would be unbearable for athletes, so the start date for the 2008 Olympics (late July) may be moved a few weeks earlier.

By contrast, on the high Tibetan Plateau temperatures are always low, and above 4,000m there is no month without frost.

VIOLENT WEATHER

Tropical storms called typhoons affect the southeast coast in late summer. These storms come from the Pacific, bringing high winds and heavy rainfall, which can cause great damage. It is difficult to predict when and where such storms are going to strike, how

CASE STUDY
2001 TYPHOONS

Seven or eight typhoons usually hit China each year. By the end of July 2001, Guangdong Province had been hit by seven typhoons. The last caused US$96 million worth of damage in three cities. While a disaster relief team helped repair homes and infrastructure and provided medical assistance, news came that yet another typhoon was on its way.

Trees are damaged as a typhoon hits the streets of Hong Kong.

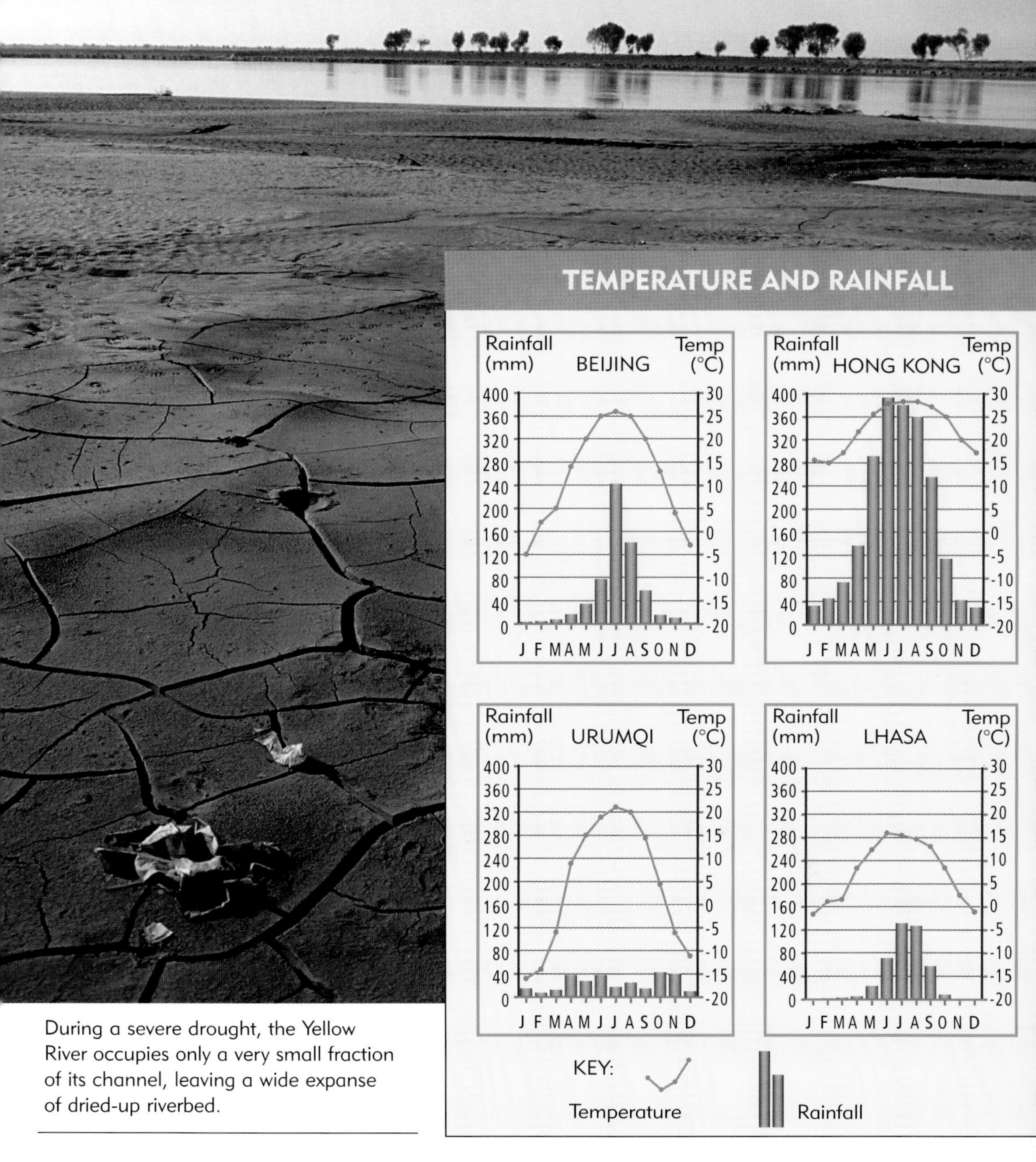

During a severe drought, the Yellow River occupies only a very small fraction of its channel, leaving a wide expanse of dried-up riverbed.

strong the winds will be and how much rain they are going to drop, even with the latest high-tech equipment. On one occasion, Hong Kong recorded 686mm of rain (more than London receives in a year) in 24 hours.

Drought

Drought is increasingly a problem in China. In 2001 even the lush middle and lower reaches of the Yangtze were experiencing drought. Northern China was particularly hard hit; by mid-June of that year only 50mm of rain had fallen. Rural areas were short of irrigation water, dry layers of soil extended down as far as 30cm and reservoirs were severely depleted. Vital food supplies of grain were lost, and farm incomes suffered. Water shortages did not just affect the large rural population: Some major cities were also short of water.

NATURAL HAZARDS

Two major natural hazards affect different parts of China: floods and earthquakes. Both occur frequently and have a serious effect on the lives and livelihoods of China's people. China has been forced to develop strategies for reducing the impact of these hazards.

ABOVE: During severe flooding in 1998, people in Jiujiang had to be rescued from their homes.

RIGHT: Workers in Dongting Lake repair dikes after the Yangtze broke its banks in 1998.

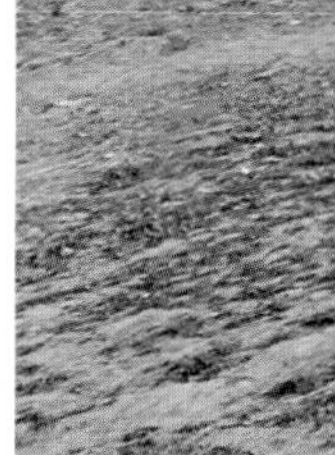

Floods

June through late September is the most likely time for flooding in China. Many rivers flood, but the Yangtze and Yellow Rivers cause more devastation than any other.

The Yangtze floods every year, but in some years the floods are more disastrous than in others. In the twentieth century there were four particularly bad floods, which occurred in 1931, 1935, 1954 and 1998. Over the past 50 years, large-scale logging in the upper reaches of the Yangtze has stripped the steep valley sides of the trees that prevented soil from being washed into the river by rain. Now, heavy rains wash loose soil into the river channel, making it shallower and reducing the amount of water the river can transport. This means that the river floods more easily.

Since 1949 the main dikes along the middle and lower reaches of major rivers have been raised and strengthened, and flood diversion projects have been built as part of flood management. But such measures along the Yangtze – especially in the Jingjiang section of the middle reaches – cannot cope with the very high floods, which tend to come once every ten years. This was the key reason for building the Three Gorges Dam (see case study page 21) and for locating the dam just before the river leaves the mountains and enters its middle course. Each year at the end of May the water level in the 660km-long reservoir will be lowered to the 145m level so that it can hold the floodwaters from the upper reaches. In October, when the flood risk passes, the water level will be raised to 175m.

CASE STUDY
FLOODING IN WUHAN

In the winter of 1997–98 there was exceptionally heavy snowfall on the Qinghai-Tibetan Plateau. This produced more snowmelt than usual in the springtime. In addition, the rains started early. Each rainstorm sent another wave of high water down the river. The worst flooding, as always, was in the middle and lower reaches of the river.

By mid-July, Wuhan, a town where flood levels reach their maximum height, was already experiencing its third flood peak. To make matters worse, Wuhan had just been deluged by a storm dumping nearly half a meter of rain in only 12 hours, so one-fifth of the city was already flooded. Weeks of anxiety followed. By then flood embankments were weakened by weeks of heavy rain. Despite efforts too reinforce them, a large number of embankments eventually failed, exposing Wuhan to still more flooding.

It was a devastating experience for those affected by it. The river rose quickly and people had to leave their homes, taking only a few possessions with them. Diseases such as cholera broke out. Businesses and factories were forced to close, transport was disrupted and power supplies were cut. Rural areas were also affected, and crops and livestock were lost. In the middle and lower reaches of the river more than 1 million hectares of land were flooded and 1,542 people were killed. Financial costs were US$80 billion.

EARTHQUAKES

Earthquakes occur frequently in many parts of China because the country lies on major fault lines and the boundaries between some of the Earth's tectonic plates. For example, the Himalayas mark the collision zone where the Indian plate, moving northward, meets the Eurasian plate.

When earthquakes occur in densely populated areas they can result in devastating loss of life and long-lasting suffering for survivors. In 2001, for example, the city of Tangshan marked the twenty-fifth anniversary of a devastating earthquake by holding a memorial service. The city's reconstruction has only recently been completed and its economy rebuilt.

Much research into earthquake activity is being undertaken in China. For example, the country's first continental scientific drillhole is located in Jiangsu Province. This probes down into an area where continental plates converge, to monitor seismic activity.

In the Jiashi earthquake many homes were reduced to rubble.

CASE STUDY
THE JIASHI EARTHQUAKE

On 24 February 2003 at 10:03 a.m. local time, a large earthquake (measuring 6.8 on the Richter scale) struck Jiashi county without any warning. Two more quakes (measuring 5.0 on the Richter scale) struck the following day. In total there were also 734 aftershocks, averaging 40 an hour. The damage was considerable: 268 people were killed, 4,000 were injured, and 8,861 homes – many made of sun-dried brick – and 17 schools were damaged. The low nighttime temperatures at this time of year caused great hardship for those sleeping outdoors. About 1,300 soldiers, 12 medical teams and 200 police officers arrived in the disaster area to conduct rescue work on 24 February, with more helpers arriving the next day. Many people had been buried under debris and rubble.

Earthquake activity occurred in the area again at the end of March and in the first week of May, resulting in five earthquakes and almost 400 aftershocks. About 60,000 to 70,000 people were made homeless.

CASE STUDY
THE KUNLUN SHAN EARTHQUAKE

Not all earthquakes cause serious damage. On 14 November 2001, a large earthquake (7.8 on the Richter scale) occurred on the northern Qinghai-Tibetan Plateau. It was the biggest quake to occur on mainland China for more than 50 years. Its epicenter was in the remote, uninhabited Kokoxili region, near the border between Qinghai Province and Xinjiang. The earthquake caused a fracture 350km long along the western end of the Kunlun fault, and 23 aftershocks occurred within one month of the event. The only damage was to some shrines along the Golmud-Lhasa highway. The new Qinghai-Tibet railway now crosses this earthquake-prone region.

EARTHQUAKE PRECAUTIONS

In areas where earthquakes are common, it is a good idea to plan ahead for when they might happen. For example, frequent earthquakes affect the province of Yunnan, so since 1985 special precautions are in place. Constructions sites are carefully checked to make sure that new building standards are being employed, such as height restrictions and the use of a new lighter but stronger brick. A disaster drill has been established, and TV campaigns and posters help to increase people's awareness of how to cope in the event of a quake.

Survivors of the earthquake in Lijiang, 1996, have their lunch outside their destroyed homes.

Some people still wear the uniform that was worn by men and women all over China before 1978.

In 1978 the Chinese leader at the time, Deng Xiaoping, decided that China needed new ideas for economic growth. He declared that "to get rich is glorious," and he began to loosen the government's control of the economy. The economic growth that Deng jump-started has led to huge changes in the lives of Chinese people. Today, employment in both industry and services is rising, while traditional jobs in agriculture are being lost at a very rapid rate.

SPECIAL ECONOMIC ZONES

China's economy has been growing briskly at a rate of roughly 8 percent per year. This rapid growth stems from the vision of China's former leader, Deng Xiaoping. By 1980, four new growth centers known as Special Economic Zones (SEZ) were being developed on the southeast coast of China. By 1984, 14 east-coast cities had been declared "open cities," which gave them the right to trade with other countries (in addition to the Soviet Union and Eastern European countries). These "open cities" were at the heart of the rapid growth in China's economy through the 1980s and 1990s.

RAPID DEVELOPMENT

Joint ventures between transnational companies (TNCs) and Chinese firms have helped to finance industrial growth in China, but much funding has also come from wealthy Chinese expatriates (people living abroad). In addition, low labor costs have encouraged many overseas firms to transfer their factories to China.

Today, the impact of economic growth can readily be seen in China's urban areas. Cranes and new skyscrapers pierce the skyline in all Chinese cities, and the distance between the urban fringe and airports has shrunk noticeably. The Western-style fast-food outlets and clothes stores now visible in the center of any big city in China show how lifestyles in the country are changing. The boom in sales of luxury cars such as Bentleys and Ferraris indicates the wealth of some entrepreneurs in Beijing, the Pearl Delta cities and Shanghai. In addition, fewer Chinese people live in extreme poverty than did so 25 years ago.

In urban areas wages have risen. This has increased consumer spending, which in turn boosts industrial output, since industry produces goods for people to buy. China has an enormous domestic market, although not all of its 1.3 billion people have spare money to spend.

TELEVISION SETS PER 1,000 PEOPLE

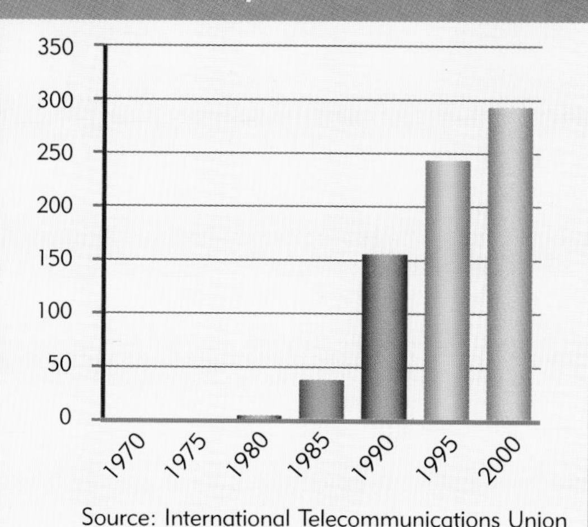

Source: International Telecommunications Union

ECONOMIC STRUCTURE, 2002 (% GDP CONTRIBUTIONS)

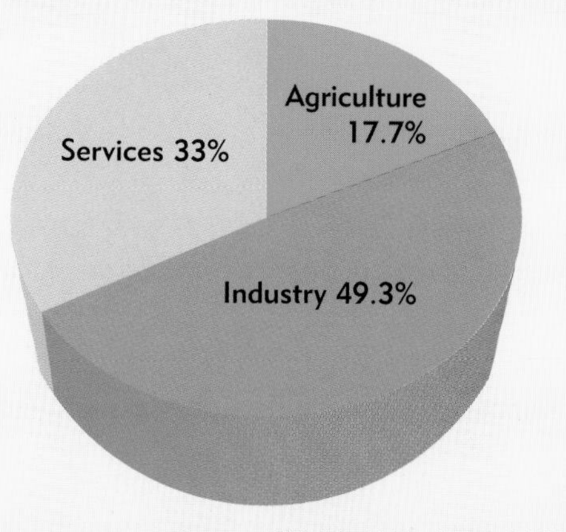

Source: *CIA World Factbook*, 2003

Uneven Growth

Economic growth has not happened uniformly throughout China. The east-coast provinces are much wealthier than the interior provinces, and urban areas are much better off than rural areas. Even some cities have a high unemployment problem. One such city is Shenyang, where the first wave of industrial development took place in the 1950s. The government, which owned all businesses at the time, developed heavy industries such as steel production. These State-Owned Enterprises (SOEs) are very inefficient and are being phased out gradually. For many of their former employees the loss of these jobs has brought great hardship. Employment in an SOE used to mean a job for life, with benefits such as housing, health care, education and a pension. But some SOEs did not give their employees severance pay, and many of the employees found themselves unable to find another job.

Gear boxes are assembled at a VW factory, in Shanghai. Private ownership of cars in China rose from 5 million in 2000 to 10 million in 2003.

ENERGY

Energy supplies are essential for economic growth. In China, new mines, factories, businesses, transport and telecommunications systems are all driving up the demand for energy. As living standards rise, so do demands for power within the home. Over the next 20 years, China will have to build many more power stations in order to avoid power shortages.

ENERGY PRODUCTION, 2003 (% OF TOTAL)

Nuclear and other fuel sources 2%

HEP 25%

Coal, oil and gas 73%

Source: *The China Business Review*, May–June 2003

ENERGY RESOURCES

In the past, China has relied on its abundant supplies of coal as its main source of energy. However, the coal's high sulfur content causes environmental damage and serious health problems. Much new energy is now generated using hydroelectric power (HEP), which is clean, cheap and renewable (it will not run out). Most hydroelectric power resources are on the upper Yangtze and its major tributaries.

China also has resources of oil and gas. However, despite being the worlds fifth-largest producer of oil, supplies are not enough to meet growing demand. China is stepping up its exploration programs for new oil and gas fields, but for now it has to import one-third of its needs. Almost half the imported oil comes from the Middle East. China needs new suppliers in order not to be dependent on oil from just one region. Russia may be able to supply oil in the future, and Indonesia and Australia supply liquid natural gas (LNG).

The oil refinery at Daqing oil fields, Heilongjiang Province.

CASE STUDY
THE THREE GORGES DAM

Five sets of parallel locks allow shipping to pass through the enormous Three Gorges Dam.

The new dam across the Yangtze River will provide flood control, improved river transport, water storage and electricity. The dam is situated at Sandouping, about 40km upstream from the city of Yichang and 30km upstream of the Gezhouba hydroelectric power station. The Three Gorges Dam is the largest power project in the world. It will supply electricity to the power-short eastern seaboard of China, to provinces in central China and to the city of Chongqing. Electricity will be available to businesses and homes in the middle Yangtze region and part of the western province of Sichuan. Sales of electricity will pay for the cost of the dam.

On 1 June 2003, the waters started to rise behind the dam, and by 10 June they had reached the 135m level. By August 2003 the first two turbines – in the left bank powerhouse – had started production and by October two more turbines were working. Plans are for four power units to be added each year. Each turbine produces enough electricity to meet the needs of a city of 1 million people. When all 26 turbines have been installed, the project will supply 10 percent of China's needs and greatly reduce air pollution. The project is expected to be completed by 2009, by which time the water in the reservoir will have risen to its maximum height of 175m.

Despite the benefits of the Three Gorges Dam, the project has been highly controversial. At least 1.2 million people have been forced to move to new homes because the old ones will be covered by the dam's waters. Environmentalists have spoken out about water pollution and loss of biodiversity (the number and variety of living things in the area). Large amounts of toxic waste from industrial plants and mines have already accumulated in the mud in the reservoir area. Before the dam was constructed, large quantities of industrial waste and sewage were carried out to sea. Many environmentalists are now concerned that this waste will not be flushed out of the reservoir. They are also worried that the habitats of the Chinese river dolphin and the finless porpoise, which are below the dam, will be affected.

CASE STUDY: SHENZHEN – A MODERN DEVELOPMENT

ABOVE: As in most of China's major cities, dramatic silvery skyscrapers dominate the skyline of downtown Shenzhen.

A good example of the rapid changes caused by Deng Xiaoping's economic reforms (see pages 18–19) is the city of Shenzhen. The first SEZ in China, Shenzhen has been transformed from a village in the Pearl River Delta in 1980 to a vibrant city with the highest GDP per capita in China in 2001. In 1980, most people in the delta area were farmers and today's industrial zone was just undeveloped land. Electricity and water supply, sewerage, housing for workers, roads and port facilities still had to be built.

Shenzhen's proximity to Hong Kong gave it a distinct advantage over other potential SEZs: Hong Kong was an important manufacturing center and needed more space. When Hong Kong businesses shifted their manufacturing to Shenzhen, they also brought managerial skills and invested significant amounts of money in the area. In return, they found cheaper workers, paid no tax for the first three years, and paid reduced customs duties and low land rents.

The first industries to develop in the area were light industries requiring a great deal of labor but few skills. Cheap plastic toys and clothing were typical products. Labor flooded in, not only from the surrounding rural area, but also from rural areas hundreds of kilometers away, such as Sichuan Province, where rural unemployment is high. Those who have migrated to Shenzhen are mostly young people, attracted by factory wages three times higher than wages in the rural areas.

By 1995 Shenzhen began to manufacture high-tech goods, and today the city is the leading center in China for such products. Computer hardware and software are produced there, and the city's 1,500 factories turn out 40 million computers per year. Surrounding small towns are also involved in the industry; for example, within a 60-minute drive of Shenzhen, Fuji Xerox can access 95 percent of all the components it needs. The high-tech sector produces 47 percent of the country's industrial output.

An impressive 15 percent of mainland China's exports come from Shenzhen. There are now 27,000 foreign investment enterprises in the city, which is home to international companies such as IBM, Compaq and Samsung, as well as the Chinese giants Legend and Kingdee. Not surprisingly Shenzhen is the biggest SEZ in China. Although Shenzhen continues to take a lead in the high-tech sector and is well known for research and development, its economy is still evolving. The service sector, for example, is growing rapidly.

Shenzhen has grown from a population of less than 25,000 in 1980 to 7 million in 2003. It is now the most important city in the Pearl River Delta (PRD), which has become one of China's key manufacturing regions. The PRD accounts for almost 7 percent of the country's Gross Domestic Product (GDP), yet has less than 3 percent of China's population.

BELOW: A billboard shows Deng and his vision for Shenzhen.

CASE STUDY: PUDONG – A FLAGSHIP DEVELOPMENT

In 1990, China launched the next stage of its program of reform and development. This time Shanghai, a long-established city, was chosen as the base. The government had two goals. The first was to make Shanghai a key international economic, trade and financial center. The second was for Shanghai to stimulate further development of the Yangtze valley, which already accounted for 40 percent of China's total industrial and agricultural output.

Shanghai's location is ideal for both roles. Located on the east coast, the city is well placed for international trade, especially with other Pacific nations. And situated at the mouth of the Yangtze, it is at the gateway to the Yangtze valley, allowing access to large areas within China.

Downtown Shanghai was far too crowded already, but the district of Pudong was still relatively undeveloped. It was the obvious choice, although bridges and tunnels had to be built to connect the two sides of the Huangpu River. Since 1990, growth has been phenomenal. Then Pudong was mainly farmland, with a few wharves along the riverbanks. Today it looks more like Manhattan, with futuristic buildings competing to be the highest on the city skyline. The Jinmao Tower at 420.5m is soon to be eclipsed by the Shanghai World Financial Center at 508.1m, which is currently under construction.

Pudong was planned in a series of zones, each concentrating on specific functions. The Lujiazui Zone (downtown) is the financial and trade center; across the river is the Bund, the old financial district of Shanghai. The other three key zones are the Jinqiao Modern Industrial Park (the largest manufacturing center in Shanghai), Zhangjiang High-tech Park, and the Waigaoqiao Free Trade Zone, which has a deep-water harbor.

LEFT: Tourists take in the futuristic view of Pudong's impressive buildings from the Bund.

BELOW: Shanghai Stock Exchange, Lujiazu, is the largest in China, monitoring over 400 companies.

Pudong has attracted more than 50 foreign investment banks, 160 overseas financial institutions and 85 leading TNCs such as Hewlett Packard, JVC, Roche and General Motors. In ten years Pudong built up its GDP from zero to one-fifth of Shanghai's total production. In 2000, Pudong also accounted for one-third of Shanghai's exports and one-third of overseas investments.

Economic development in Shanghai has increased with the success of Pudong, where priority is now being given to new and high-tech industries. In 2005 information technology will be the number-one industry. Soon the three key industrial development zones will be clustered within a single high-tech belt.

Residential areas have also been developed, with new educational, health care, cultural and sports facilities. Shopping malls and supermarkets, an aquarium, restaurants and the Huaxia Tourist Zone (which offers a wide variety of leisure pursuits) cater to the residents of Pudong, as well as people from other districts of Shanghai and farther afield.

LEISURE AND TOURISM

Before the 1980s leisure and tourism scarcely existed in China. Tourism, however, is an excellent way to boost economic growth, making demands on other sectors of the economy such as industry, agriculture and transport. So in 2000, China's public holidays – May 1 (Labor Day) and October 1 (National Day) – were each extended to a week. Added to the week-long Chinese Spring Festival, many people in China now enjoy three weeks' vacation per year. These holidays are called the "Golden Weeks." The introduction of the Golden Weeks immediately increased income from tourism, which in 2001 was up 10.9 percent on the previous year.

Longer holidays enable Chinese people to learn more about their country, increasing understanding between China's different ethnic groups. And when tourists visit remote areas, it brings the local people in touch with the modern way of life. Tourists also bring money to areas that have no resources other than scenery or culture. With its many tourist attractions such as diverse landscapes and cultural heritage, China is also attracting an increasing number of overseas visitors.

CASE STUDY
SCENIC TOURISM: CRUISING THE LI RIVER

One of China's most spectacular attractions is the landscape of towerlike hills, known as the karst landscape, of the Li River valley, in Guangxi Province. There, heavy tropical rainfall and acids from decaying vegetation have dissolved the limestone, creating both conical and towerlike hills. The hills rise spectacularly from the river's floodplain. The rain has also dissolved the limestone within the hills, producing enormous caverns with stalactites, stalagmites and passages. Waterfalls link passages cut at different levels.

The floodplain of the Li River also attracts tourists, who come to see the picturesque rice paddies, water buffalo and bamboo groves. Another popular sight is the cormorant fishermen, who use the trained water birds to catch and retrieve their fish.

Stunning karst scenery dominates the landscape along the route of the Li River, in Guangxi Province.

THEME PARKS

In the 1990s theme parks became the rage in China, and are still extremely popular. Shenzhen is the theme park capital. With several theme parks, it is China's third-most-popular tourist destination. China Folklore Village, comprising 24 villages and representing 21 ethnic groups, has taken ten years to build. It is a big attraction in a city where 98 percent of the population originated from different parts of China. The Splendid China Scenic Area not only has miniature replicas of scenery, but it also houses replicas of historic sites. Despite higher incomes, not many Chinese people can afford to travel abroad: Shenzhen's World Miniature theme park enables them to see some of the world's most famous buildings.

Visitors enjoy a day out at the Happy Kingdom High-tech Amusement Park in Shenzhen.

LEISURE MAP

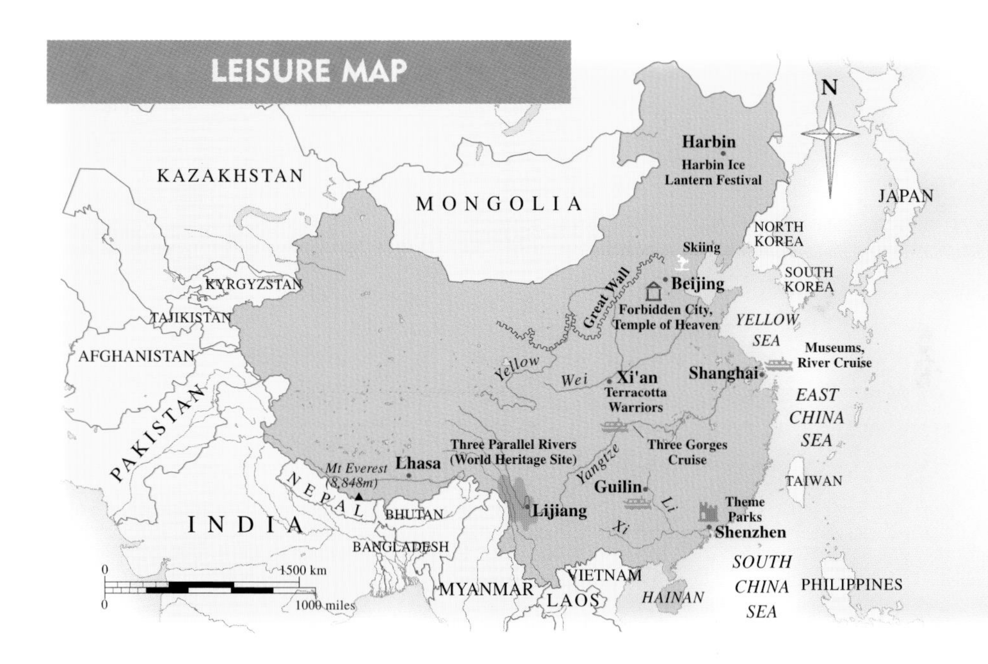

WINTER SPORTS

For the wealthy, the latest trend in leisure activities is winter sports; there are eight ski slopes around Beijing, for example. In the north, winters are cold enough for snow, especially in the mountains. Even in the southwest people can count on there being snow in the high mountains during winter. In addition, the Chinese have experimented with cloud seeding: producing snow for ski slopes by sending up rockets loaded with silver iodide. Silver iodide helps the formation of ice crystals, which turn into snowflakes. One experiment in 2000 was so successful that traffic in Beijing was halted by heavy snowfall.

Every day, thousands of tourists flock to see the Great Wall of China, easily the country's biggest attraction.

The Great Wall of China

The Great Wall is China's biggest tourist attraction. There are several points along its 6,430-km length where it is possible to view the Great Wall clearly. One of the most popular is at Badaling, 75km northwest of Beijing. A purpose-built expressway makes the journey from Beijing possible in about an hour, and a gigantic parking lot was opened in 2001.

Gazing along the Great Wall winding across the high mountains gives the onlooker a tremendous sense of history. The wall was built in sections over a long period of time, with most of it dating from the Ming dynasty (1368–1644). However, about a third of this famous landmark has already been lost and another third is badly damaged. The long-term weathering effects of rain and ice have partly caused this damage. Even though the wall at Badaling is relatively young (only 600 years old), part of it has had to be rebuilt.

Modern times have placed extra pressures on the Great Wall. Vandalism has become an increasing problem, for example, and the 10 million people visiting the wall each year have also taken their toll, slowly damaging the structure they have come to see. On busy days the wall is so crowded it is almost impossible to move. One way the authorities have tried to help preserve the Great Wall is by limiting commercial activities. For instance, cafes and theme parks have to be built at least half a kilometer away.

The Terracotta Warriors

The terracotta warriors are China's second most popular tourist site, with over 2 million tourists visiting each year – one quarter of them coming from overseas. Coping with such large numbers is like moving a modern-day army, so the whole process needs to be highly organized. A new international terminal has been built at Xi'an airport to handle foreign visitors, many of whom spend only one night

in Xi'an, as part of a two-week tour of China. The hotels ensure guests' speedy departure by bus to the Terracotta Museum, about an hour's drive away.

Tourism has brought new wealth not only to hotel staff and others employed directly in the industry, but also to all the other people involved in the tourism supply chain in Xi'an. For example, tourism has benefited the local rural population. Outside the museum complex, people work as stall-holders selling souvenirs and food. Inside there are jobs as guides in the museum and the three pits containing the discoveries, or as staff in the restaurant or shop. The farmer who made the discovery even makes money signing guidebooks bought by the tourists.

The downside of the growth in tourism is the damage to the clay statues. Once brightly colored, with exposure to the light they soon became just a dull yellow. More serious still, the statues are at risk from mold caused by the breath and body heat of so many visitors.

ORIGIN OF FOREIGN TOURISTS

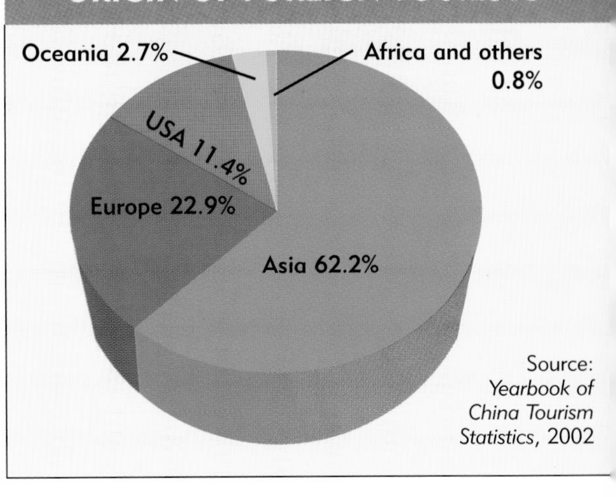

Source: *Yearbook of China Tourism Statistics*, 2002

DISCOVERING AN ANCIENT ARMY

In 1974, farmers sinking a new well in Shaanxi Province made a remarkable discovery. They found a set of three burial pits containing pieces of terracotta warriors and bronze weapons, which proved to be part of a major archaeological site dating back to the Qin dynasty (221–206 B.C.). The warriors were put in the burial pits to protect Emperor Qin from attack in the afterlife. The warriors are a major Chinese tourist attraction.

The terracotta warriors: So far more than 6,000 armored warriors and horses have been found.

FARMING

Farming is the traditional way of life in China. It has always been hard work and today much of the land is still tilled by hand. In total, only 10 percent of China is suitable for growing crops. Almost everywhere, people work small plots of land, of roughly the same size. Imagine a farm only a quarter of a hectare – a quarter of the size of a football field! Feeding 22 percent of the world's population (1.3 billion people) on only 7 percent of the world's arable land is a major challenge. Climate largely dictates which crops can be grown in different parts of China.

In the mountainous regions, terraced hillsides provide flat land for growing crops.

MAIN FARMING AREAS

The North China Plain is the largest area of flat, fertile land in the country. Vast areas are now under irrigation, which is very important because the summer rainfall in this area is often not enough for crop growth.

The plains of the middle and lower Yangtze and the Pearl River Delta are intensively farmed. With warmer winters than farther north, the land in this region can yield two harvests each year. The hot, wet summers mean that rice is the most important grain. In the Yangtze region wheat, barley and rapeseed are grown in winter. Farther south, the winter is warm enough to grow a second rice crop.

The other important farming area is the fertile Chengdu Plain, where a 2,200-year-old irrigation system makes it possible to sustain intensive farming.

CHANGES IN FARMING

Farming in China has been undergoing change in recent years. Better seeds, fertilizers, and increased use of irrigation (essential where annual rainfall is less than 400mm) have increased output, as have better skills and technical support for farmers. Rice occupies 25 percent of the cropland, and a new hybrid rice

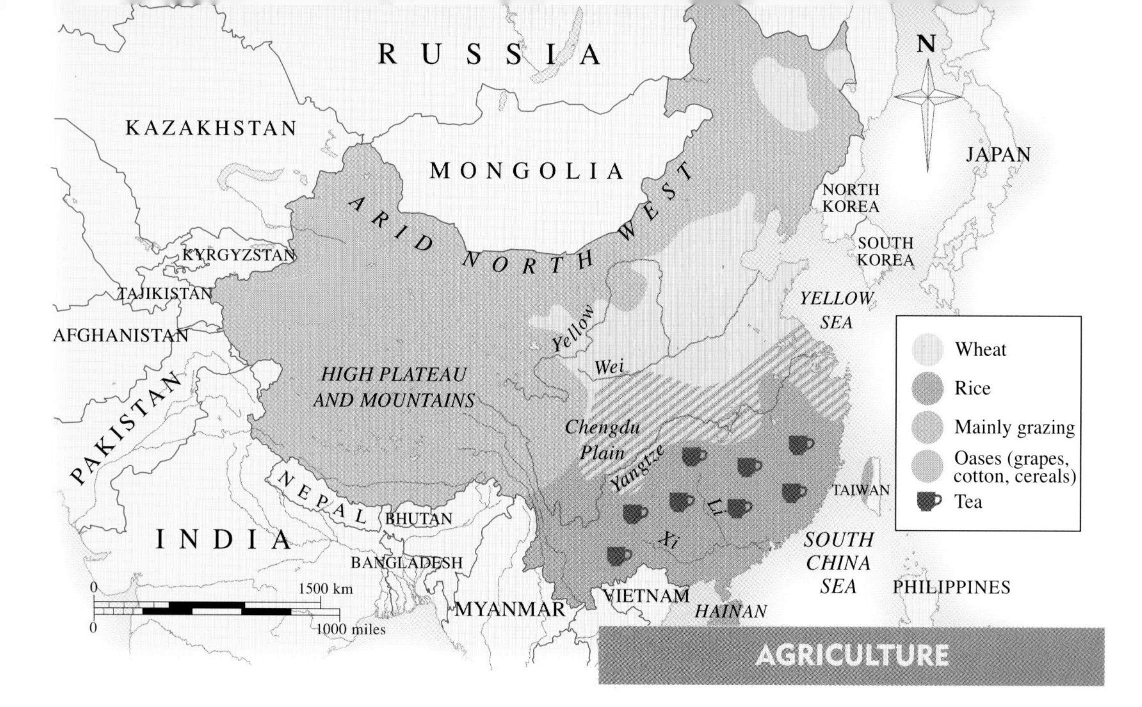

has boosted crop yields. But while crop yields improve, good farmland is being lost as urban growth and reservoirs crowd out farmers. Ironically, the reservoirs often provide water for irrigation.

Economic reforms have permitted farmers to grow crops such as fruits and vegetables for sale at market, alongside the quota of grain they are required to sell to the government. Changing lifestyles, especially in the city, mean that eating habits are changing, too. In urban areas more wealthy people can buy a greater variety of foods, not simply staple foods such as rice. Meat, especially lean cuts, forms an increasingly large part of Chinese people's diets; so do eggs, poultry and vegetable oils. Farmers near urban centers are therefore growing higher-value crops for sale in the cities. Aquaculture (the farming of fish for sale) is increasing in popularity. Often the fish are grown in flooded rice paddies.

HIGH-TECH FARMING METHODS

Bioengineering and IT are being used to help increase China's food production. In Pudong, a third of the district is to be kept for high-tech, market-oriented agribusiness, which China would like to see develop further. Agribusiness is commercial farming using up-to-date technology, such as computer-controlled greenhouses to produce vegetables and flowers, and mechanized rice harvesting on large fields. This is very different from traditional farming methods, which are labor intensive, using small plots of land to produce just enough food for the farmers to feed themselves.

Workers check their nets at a fish farm in Shaoxing.

Many farmers in rural areas hand-till small plots of land with the help of water buffalo.

RURAL AREAS

While China's cities have become more prosperous, rural areas have lagged behind. In fact, the gap between rural and urban standards of living has widened. Rural wages average only one-third of urban earnings, and although the number of rural poor has decreased, many people in the countryside still live in poverty.

Farming is in crisis: There are far too many farmers and too little land. Often the land is not very productive. Steep-sided mountains, which are common in China, are difficult and time-consuming to work on. On the upper slopes, cooler, wetter weather and poor soil reduce crop yields. Where steep slopes have been used for crops, soils are washed away during heavy rainfall. Moreover, farmers are faced with the possibility of flooding, drought, pests or disease. Add to these problems the low selling-price of grain crops, and it is easy to see how difficult it is for Chinese farmers to make a living.

To boost their incomes, some farmers spend part of the year in off-farm employment. Local industries called Town and Village Enterprises (TVEs) have provided many of these jobs. Several members of a family may work in local TVEs. Earnings from such work often exceed farming incomes.

MOVEMENT TO CITIES

There are not enough jobs for all the people living in the countryside, and many farmers leave to work in distant towns. Despite this movement of people, China's rural population continues to grow. There may be as many as 150 million farmworkers; that is more than half the US population. Each year, an estimated 4 million leave the land, and this figure is expected to rise in the near future.

CASE STUDY
FARMERS OF BAIMA VILLAGE

The 700 residents of Baima, a village on the Chengdu Plain, are among the more fortunate rural dwellers. In summer, rice and corn occupy most fields, but fruit, eggplants, cucumbers and other vegetables are grown as well. These find a ready market in the nearby rural town, Dujiangyan. In winter, the main crops are wheat, rapeseed (which is pressed for oil) and sweet potatoes.

Encouraged by the town government in 1993, one farmer volunteered to switch to growing kiwi fruit (though he kept his pigs, chickens and ducks as an insurance against failure). The kiwi fruit are sold in the local market, and the gamble of changing crops has paid off. With his increased income the farmer has been able to support three people and move to a bigger house. If a market can be found for the kiwi fruit in Japan, the crop could become extremely profitable.

Some farmers in Baima earn extra money by working in the village factory, making coal-dust briquettes, the main domestic fuel. Others have jobs in nearby Dujiangyan, a growing tourist attraction. People from the villages around Dujiangyan also seek work in Chengdu, only half an hour's bus ride on the new expressway linking the two towns.

Making bricks using local clay is another way for rural people to supplement their incomes. This small-scale brick-making enterprise is in Guizhou.

DEVELOPING THE WEST

China's western region is a vast and sparsely populated area. The government has developed long-term plans to address the west's underdevelopment, high levels of poverty and poor communications.

Chongqing, already an important city, has been selected to be a leader in economic development. The city is expanding and its center is undergoing regeneration. New industrial areas are springing up and its infrastructure is being upgraded.

DEVELOPING NATURAL RESOURCES

Taking advantage of local natural resources – minerals, water, land and scenery – is a way of creating wealth in this vast region. Most of China's mineral resources are in the west, and in the last 10 years, 23 oilfields have been developed in the Tarim Basin. A 3,800km pipeline is being planned to take natural gas from the basin to Shanghai, and nearby Korla has been transformed into a large modern city.

The enormous water resources of the upper Yangtze are only now being developed for HEP, and water is to be transferred into the Yellow River to reduce water shortages on the North China Plain. Shortages of land in the crowded east have led some large industrial firms to set up factories in the western regions. For example, the Tunhe tomato ketchup plant in Xinjiang is China's largest ketchup exporter.

Lijiang Old Town: The traditional way of life is disappearing with the growth of tourism.

Tourism

Tourism is seen as a way of bringing remote peoples in touch with modern life. It is also a way of helping the majority Han Chinese to understand the culture of China's ethnic minorities (see page 37). Both concepts are important in opening up the west. With the building of new airports, such as Lijiang's in 1997, Yunnan Province has begun to attract tourists. They come to see the spectacular scenery and Yunnan's cultural attractions.

Transport

The distance from Kashgar, near the western border of Xinjiang, to Beijing is 4,000km. But distance is only part of the problem. Plateaux and high mountains make up most of the region, and deserts mark the northern edge. Not surprisingly, there are few transport links, particularly with the rest of China.

Over the last decade new roads, railways and airports have been constructed in the region. Not yet completed are the highway from northwest Yunnan to Lhasa and the Golmud–Lhasa section of the Qinghai-Tibet Railway. The railway, the highest in the world, has presented several challenges. The toughest has been the 550km stretch that runs over permafrost, where track laying and tunneling are extremely difficult; it took 40 years to invent the technology to do this. For construction workers, the oxygen-poor air imposes physical limits, and in winter all work has to stop because of the intense cold. By July 2007 the entire project is due to be finished and Tibet will have its first railway.

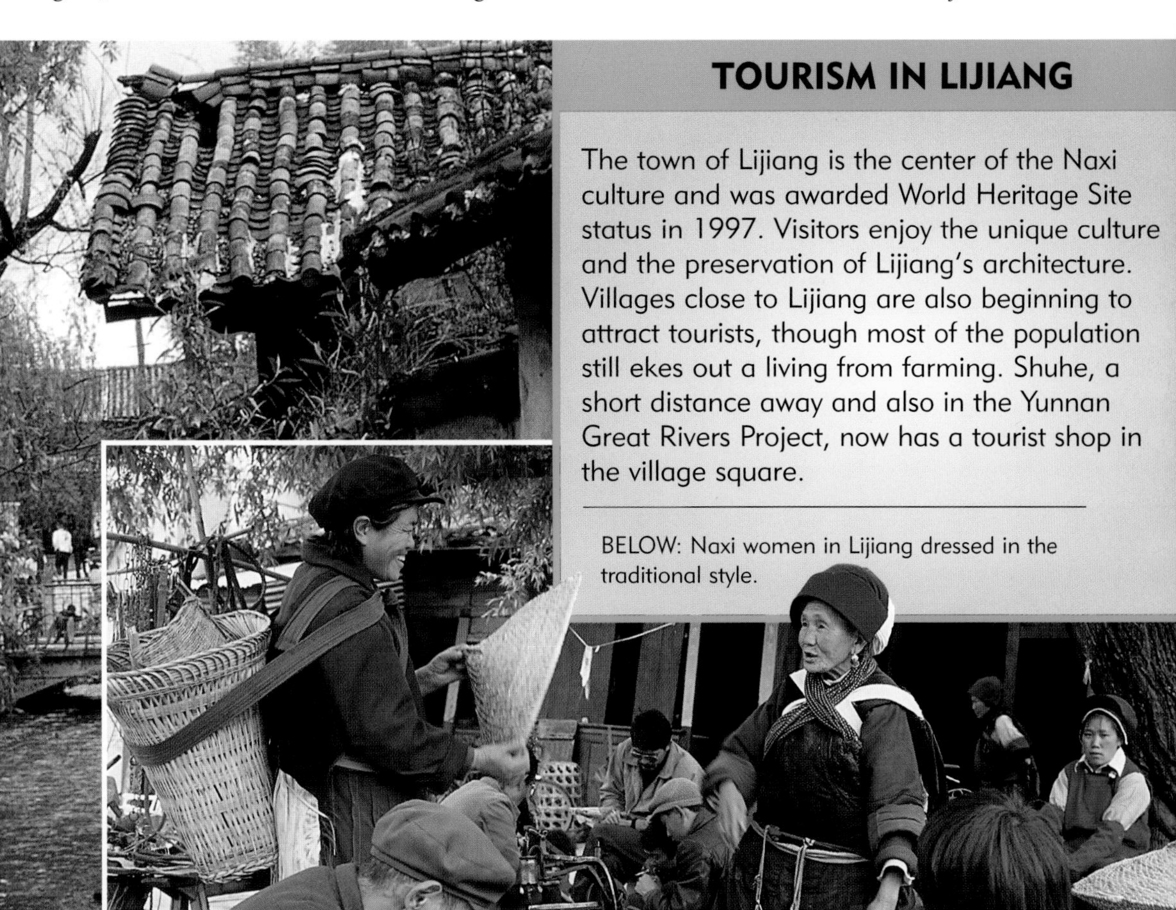

TOURISM IN LIJIANG

The town of Lijiang is the center of the Naxi culture and was awarded World Heritage Site status in 1997. Visitors enjoy the unique culture and the preservation of Lijiang's architecture. Villages close to Lijiang are also beginning to attract tourists, though most of the population still ekes out a living from farming. Shuhe, a short distance away and also in the Yunnan Great Rivers Project, now has a tourist shop in the village square.

BELOW: Naxi women in Lijiang dressed in the traditional style.

Due to changes in government policies, one-child families are now the norm for China.

China has the world's largest population – 1.3 billion – and this figure is still growing. All these people need a constant supply of food, water, minerals and energy, as well as housing, education, health care and pensions.

Population Growth and Challenges

Since 1949, China's population has grown rapidly, doubling between 1949 and 1987. The years 1964 to 1974 witnessed a baby boom, with an additional 200 million people being born. China's government wanted to raise living standards in the country – a difficult enough challenge without the population growing by 13 million people each year.

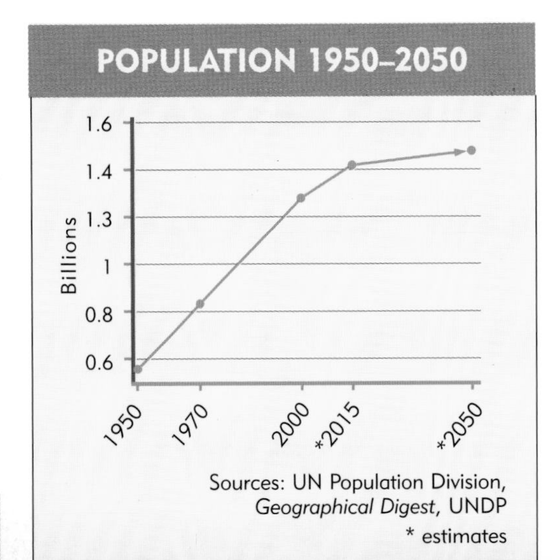

Controlling Population Growth

The baby boom prompted the introduction of family planning policies in China. In the 1970s, people were encouraged to marry later and have fewer children. But these measures did not reduce the population growth rate as the government hoped, and in 1980 China adopted a one-child policy, whereby each couple is allowed to have only one child. Financial rewards and penalties were used to encourage couples to adhere to the policy. Access to education and health care, for example, were available for only one child.

Couples in urban areas have tended to comply with the one-child policy. But in rural areas the policy is not always followed. Health care and education benefits are not always available in rural areas, even for one child, so there is less incentive for parents to comply. Parents also often feel they need a large family to help them on the farm.

Impacts of Family Planning

In China as a whole, the one-child policy is reducing population growth. Between 1980 and 2000, the policy averted more than 300 million births, and the growth rate is now only 0.88 percent. If this growth rate remains constant, by 2040 China's population should peak at just over 1.4 billion people, and by 2099 it should have declined to 800 million.

This shrinking population brings its own problems, however. China now has a higher proportion of older people than ever before, and this will increase further as the "baby boomers" head toward retirement age. With fewer young people to support the elderly, providing pensions and care for seniors has become a growing concern, and residential homes for the elderly are now springing up. The one-child policy has created other social problems. Single children are sometimes spoiled, and these children have become known as "Little Emperors." There is also a growing number of juvenile delinquents in China.

ETHNIC MINORITIES

There are 56 ethnic groups in China. The largest group is the Han, who make up 92 percent of the population. The one-child policy does not apply to China's ethnic minority groups – 104 million people – and their growth rate is 3.5 percent a year.

SOCIAL INDICATORS

UNDER-FIVE MORTALITY RATE

Deaths per thousand births

250
225
200
175
150
125
100
75
50
25

1960
1970
1980
1990
2001

Sources: UNICEF, UNDP and World Bank

LIFE EXPECTANCY (YEARS)

Age

80
70
60
50
40

1960
1970
1980
1990
2000

Source: Social Watch (February 2003)

People jostle for space on the crowded streets of Shanghai.

POPULATION DISTRIBUTION

China's population is very unevenly distributed. Most people live in China's eastern and central provinces, which make up just under half the country's area. Even within this area, population densities vary: Most people live in places that have water, flat land and fertile soils. These are also the regions that the government has favored for economic growth, providing job opportunities for the people who live there and attracting migrants from other parts of China.

More than 25 percent of China's population (about 325 million people) live on the North China Plain, where rural densities exceed 400 people per km^2. The Yangtze Delta is home to 100 million people, giving an average density close to 1,000 inhabitants per km^2, but in some areas densities are more than 75,000 people per km^2. In parts of the Pearl River Delta, densities reach 40,000 per km^2.

However, in arid and semiarid areas, population numbers drop dramatically and densities are low, usually lower than 1 person per km^2. The high plateaux, mountains and arid regions of China discourage settlement. In Tibet, for example, thin soils, harsh winters and short, damp summers restrict development and therefore job opportunities. Only in some valleys is it possible to grow a few crops, and for most people yak herding is their only livelihood. In Qinghai, most of which is covered with grassland, there are more animals than people. In arid Xinjiang, larger settlements have developed only where irrigation is possible or where minerals such as oil and gas can be extracted.

POPULATION STRUCTURE (2001)

MALE
FEMALE
80+
75–79
70–74
65–69
60–64
55–59
50–54
45–49
40–44
35–39
30–34
25–29
20–24
15–19
10–14
5–9
0–4
70 60 50 40 30 20 10 0
0 10 20 30 40 50 60 70
Millions

Source: US Census Bureau, International Database

POPULATION DISTRIBUTION

About 15 million people live in the city of Shanghai. Many residents live in cramped, overcrowded accommodation.

Countryside Dwellers

About 64 percent of China's population still live in the countryside. Just a few decades ago the proportion was much higher. While the proportion of people living in rural areas has dropped, due to population growth the actual number living in the countryside has, in fact, risen from 896 million in 1990 to 934 million in 2001. Rural settlements are mainly villages but there are also small towns.

City Dwellers

Urban settlement is predominantly in eastern China, and the largest cities are either coastal or near the coast. Since 1984, urban growth has been very rapid. The largest concentration of cities is in the Yangtze Delta, which has more than 50 towns and cities, together containing 55 million people. These lie mainly along the 250km-long transport corridors north and south of the Yangtze River. Shanghai, Nanjing and Hangzhou are the key cities. The Pearl River Delta has a smaller concentration of towns and cities. Guangzhou, Shenzhen and Hong Kong together have a population of over 28 million.

At 1.6 million km^2, Xinjiang is China's largest province, but its population is only 18 million.

Migrants work on a construction site in Zhongshan, Guangdong Province.

MIGRATION AND URBANIZATION

Between 1991 and 1999, the number of cities in China increased from 479 to 667. The size of the cities also grew. Already China has 13 cities with over 2 million inhabitants. The Asian Development Bank estimates that by 2010 China's urban population will have increased from 360 million to 700 million – almost double its current size. This means that about half of China's population will be urban; by 2050, 75 percent of the population could be living in towns and cities.

CHANGING SOCIETY

Until Deng's economic reforms were enacted, very few people moved from the countryside to the cities. A system of household registration known as *hukou* had been introduced under communist rule to prevent an influx to the towns. Every person in China has an identity card stating his or her place of birth, and a person is entitled to official housing, education and health care only in this area.

In 1984 this *hukou* system became less strict. And as the economy started to grow, it created new jobs, providing much-needed employment opportunities for unemployed rural workers. Large numbers of people left the countryside in search of work in the towns and cities. Today, China has a large migrant or "floating" population of roughly 100 million people.

MIGRANT LABOR

Migrant workers tend to get only second-rate jobs – particularly dirty jobs that no one else wants. Cities such as Beijing and Shanghai (each with about 3 million floating workers) even bar migrants from getting certain jobs, especially managerial posts. Migrants tend to be employed in shoe, clothing, and furniture factories, on construction sites, or in domestic service. Competition for jobs with unemployed urban residents has led some cities to limit the number of migrants.

Migrant workers are paid less, $549 a year compared with the average urban wage of $994. Also, many do not receive their full due. Often wages are paid only once a year, at the Chinese New Year, and some of the money is withheld until workers return after the holiday. Finally, many migrants work in conditions that are dangerous, and some have suffered injuries at work that leave them unemployable in the future. Social security measures are gradually being introduced to help migrant workers.

In 2002, more than 13 million people from the province of Sichuan were migrant workers. Nearly half of these workers were living outside the province. Most migrants move to towns where relatives or neighbors have

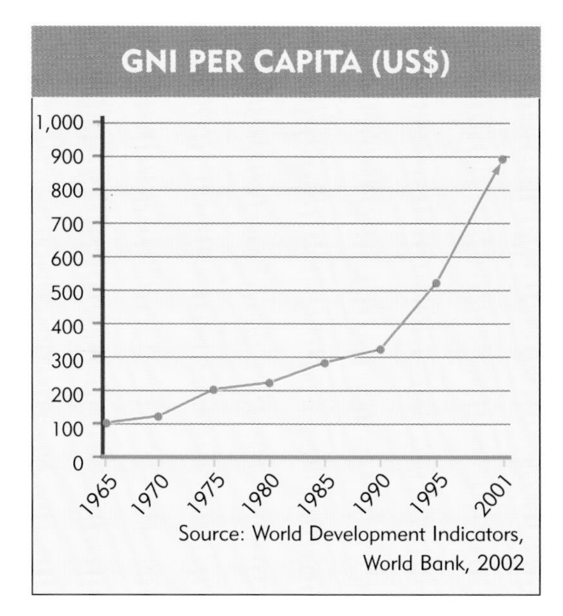

found them a job. Anhui Province is now setting up agencies to train workers in various skills and help them migrate to jobs in six of the major cities. Migrants send back more than $44 billion a year to Anhui. This arrangement solves local unemployment and brings money to the local economy. In total, rural villages receive $824 billion each year from workers who live elsewhere. Some returning migrants use their earnings to set up businesses using their new skills.

MOVE TO THE CITIES

China is now planning for the transfer of an estimated 200 million rural workers to the cities between 2000 and 2010. Providing housing, schools and transport for these extra workers is going to be very costly.

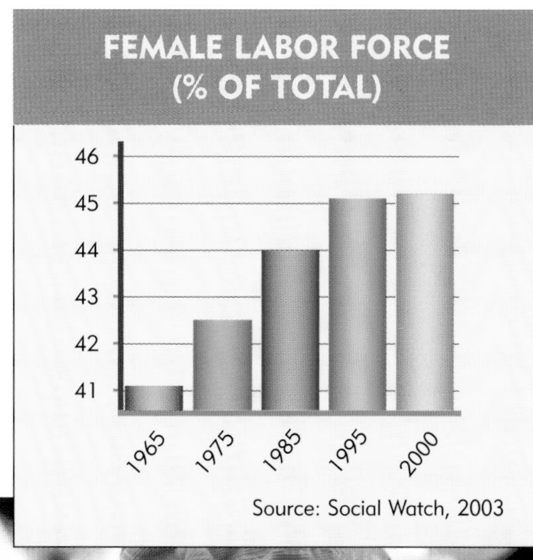

These migrant women are working in a doll factory, close to Shenzhen, Guangdong Province.

LIFE IN THE CITIES

Large areas of China's major cities are like gigantic construction sites. The old city centers are undergoing regeneration, and residential and office towers seem to spring up almost overnight. New industrial sites for high-tech industries and developing transport networks also form part of the rapid growth. The speed of this urban growth is causing social problems such as housing shortages, unemployment, traffic congestion, and strains on the health and education services.

BEIJING

For many urban dwellers the quality of life has greatly improved over the last 20 years. In Beijing, new residential areas offer more spacious accommodation, with all the comforts of modern living. People who live in the city have higher incomes and access to education, social welfare and leisure activities. The most expensive housing is at the edge of the city, away from the worst congestion.

Some of central Beijing's remaining traditional housing is being renovated and modernized. Much of it, however, has now been demolished. The former residents have moved to new housing developments on the city outskirts. To make the city "greener," the government has planned green areas, tree-lined roads and a large new city park. These will increase green space in the city, improving the urban environment.

In Beijing's center is a modern central business district (CBD). There are far more residential buildings here than in CBDs in wealthier countries, but the main street also has banks, offices, shops and leisure facilities such as fitness centers, bars, restaurants, and cultural and arts centers. The CBD is not far from Beijing's two major tourist attractions, the Forbidden City and Tiananmen Square. The square is the focal point around which the

CHANGES IN QUALITY OF LIFE

	1990	2001
GDP	$425	$800
Per capita housing space	6.7m²	10.8m²
Households with electrical appliances	18.6%	98.3%

Source: *Beijing Review*, October 24, 2002

RIGHT: Chaos at a road junction as thousands of people take to their bicycles during rush hour.
BELOW: The portrait of the communist leader Mao Zedong still hangs outside the Gateway of Heavenly Peace in Beijing.

main public buildings are grouped and is also the venue for major public events.

A city of 13 million people generates many problems. One challenge is the disposal of 11,000 tonnes of garbage a day. Air pollution is another major problem. There are many polluting industries located in central Beijing, and traffic emissions add to the pollution levels. To make matters worse, in spring choking dust storms cover the city for several days at a time (see page 55). As a condition of being permitted to host the 2008 Olympics, Beijing must address its air pollution problem.

Getting to work in Beijing is becoming increasingly difficult. About ten years ago, 58 percent of all journeys were made by bicycle. Today the figure is closer to 40 percent. As people now live farther from where they work, the number of commuters has increased. Traffic often comes to a standstill.

By 2003 Beijing got its first incineration plant. Polluting industries are being moved out of central Beijing. Buses and taxis form part of the public transport system, and by 2008 about 90 percent of buses and 60 percent of taxis will have switched from diesel to natural gas, reducing traffic emissions. Mass-transit systems – subway and light rail – are being extended to the new suburbs.

TELECOMMUNICATIONS DATA

Mainline Phones	135,000,000
Mobile Phones	65,000,000
Internet Service Providers	3

Source: *CIA World Factbook*, 2003

PERSONAL COMPUTERS PER 1,000 PEOPLE

Source: World Development Indicators, World Bank

Shanghai is the undisputed first city of the Yangtze Delta, and increasing numbers of people are moving into the metropolitan area. By 2020, the population is predicted to rise to 16 million residents, with 8 million living in the central city. In order to cope with growth over the period 1999–2020, the Shanghai Municipal People's Government put in place a coordinated plan for the whole of the Shanghai metropolitan region.

People enjoying early morning t'ai chi by the Bund is a familiar sight in Shanghai.

THE CENTRAL CITY

The central city area is bounded by the Outer Ring Road. As part of the plan for the metropolitan region, a new CBD has been built in Lujiazui (Pudong). In the old downtown area, high-rise commercial buildings have replaced old housing; the original residents have been moved to the outskirts and to Pudong. The former racecourse is now a public space occupied by Renmin Park and Renmin Square, the site of new public buildings such as the museum, theater and urban planning center.

Within the Inner Ring Road, administration, finance, commerce, and cultural and tourist activities will be the most important employers. Farther out from the center will be modern high-tech industries and non-polluting industries. About 20 residential areas are to be built as well.

Densification (fitting a high density of people and activities into a limited area) is the key feature of most new developments. Shanghai's tall, futuristic high-rise buildings house a range of functions.

Shanghai is paying great attention to the urban environment. The Huangpu River and Suzhou Creek are currently being cleaned up, and these areas will function as green "corridors" within Shanghai. Parks and small gardens will increase Shanghai's green space to 7m^2 per person, improving the urban ecological environment. Also, a greenbelt is planned to surround the central city.

SATELLITE TOWNS

In order to prevent central Shanghai from becoming too big, and to make good use of the various resources available, planners will build 11 new satellite towns (separate towns near the main city and closely related to it). Each town will have one main function, for example administration, industry or transport. In addition to these satellite towns, future plans include 22 central rural towns (these are larger and more developed than rural towns), 80 rural towns and numerous villages.

URBAN TRANSPORT

Within the Inner Ring Road, the city's roads are laid out on a grid system. Farther from the center, roads are organized into ring roads and radial roads. The radial roads link satellite towns and the central city. A system of major expressways with long elevated sections is in place. These allow traffic to move at speeds of 80–120kph.

Many people in the inner city travel to work using the subway or light rail systems (opened in 2000). Many others cycle to work, but bikes are barred from some areas of the central city to reduce congestion. Eventually, 16 bridges and tunnels will link both sides of the river.

A new ferry service started up in July 2002, adding yet another means of crossing the river. By 2004 magnetic levitation or Maglev trains (which "hover" above a magnetic guide rail) connected Lujiazui to Pudong airport.

Nanpu Bridge is one of the new bridges linking the new Pudong district and old Shanghai.

TRANSPORT AND TRADE

Minor airports such as Magshi play an important role in connecting the many remote parts of China.

China is a vast country, and people travel across it in a variety of ways. Raw materials and goods also have to be transported from place to place using a number of different methods. In addition, China now trades with other countries, and its international transport links are becoming increasingly important.

GETTING AROUND

Improving China's transport network is a big challenge in a country where so much of the land is mountainous and there are many wide rivers to bridge. Linking major cities, ports, industrial areas, and resources is essential to economic development. In particular, the government is increasing links between the coastal region and the interior.

Roads

Over the past ten years, new roads have been built to link major cities. These roads now seem empty of traffic compared with roads in Europe or the United States, but they have been built with future traffic demand in mind. By 2010, the highway network will be more than 35,000km long. A new highway linking Beijing to Hong Kong is also planned.

One particular challenge is building the new highway into Tibet. Construction is now taking place in the high plateau. Temperatures there are so cold that work can be undertaken only in the summer months, so progress has been forced to slow down. The highway will eventually connect Lhasa with the rest of China.

Railways

China's railways run on a mix of steam, diesel and electric power and are an important method of transport in the country. Both long-distance and local trains carry increasingly large numbers of passengers. Freight trains are used for the long-distance transport of agricultural products as well as bulky, low-value raw materials for industry. Over 50 percent of all freight is carried by rail in China. In Europe the figure is just 15 percent.

The rail network is still growing, and it is expanding to take in mountain and desert regions in the western provinces. These regions pose special construction challenges. The recently completed Chengdu-Kunming line, for example, has over 200 tunnels. Some are so close together that the front and back portions of a train can be in different tunnels at the same time.

Air Travel

Because of the enormous distances between destinations, engineering challenges, the costs of road and rail construction, and travel time, air transport has many advantages. Air passenger traffic is likely to increase by at least 8 percent a year between now and 2021.

To cope with the growth in air transport, China plans a system dominated by three major hubs: Beijing, Shanghai and Guangdong. These three places will handle two-thirds of all passenger traffic. In addition, seven key regional hubs in the interior will each be linked to small feeder airports. In total, 118 new airports, most of them small, are planned.

Stocking up for a long journey. Railway staff sell food and drink to passengers as they board the train.

IMPACT OF TRANSPORT ON TRADE

China's international trade is currently growing. China trades with other Asian countries and, increasingly, with countries farther away, in Europe and North America. China's 2001 entry into the World Trade Organization (WTO) showed that China had become one of the world's major trading countries.

WATERWAYS

China's trade depends heavily on waterborne transport, both within the country and overseas. Water transport is the cheapest and easiest way of moving bulky raw materials, and containers loaded with goods are also moved within China by boat.

The Yangtze is by far China's most important waterway. The river is a vital link between the east and west of the country. The Yangtze and its tributaries provide 70,000km of navigable waterway, which is two-thirds of the country's total.

As well as water traffic on large rivers, simple, small boats provide vital local links on China's numerous rivers, both large and small.

PORTS

Most of China's overseas trade goes through Shanghai, Ningbo, Shenzhen, and Hong Kong (the largest container port in the world). Shanghai handles 250 million tonnes of cargo a year and is China's second-largest container port. The city is soon likely to become the world's fourth-largest container port. It has already extended its deep-water facilities by building new container terminals in Pudong, but access is restricted to 50,000-tonne ships. On Yanshan Island, south of Pudong, a deep-water harbor is being constructed, with

NEW DEVELOPMENTS

The Yangtze's importance will increase in 2009, when the water in the Three Gorges Dam reservoir reaches 175m (see page 21). At this water level, navigation hazards above Yichang, such as sandbanks and rapids, will be submerged. At the same time, a flight of five sets of parallel locks will enable two-way traffic to pass through the dam. Barges of up to 10,000 tonnes will be able to reach Chongqing for most of the year.

The Yangtze is a major shipping route within China. Cargoes range from raw materials such as wood to cars and containers.

50 berths capable of accommodating the latest container vessels. An eight-lane bridge, 32km long, will connect the port to Shanghai's new satellite town in the southeast. The whole project is scheduled for completion by 2015.

As well as the four main international ports, a string of minor ports stretches along China's east coast.

TRADE AND TRADING PARTNERS

In 2001 China's imports and exports still formed a small proportion of total world trade (4 percent and 4.3 percent respectively). However, entry into the World Trade Organization (WTO) that year caused a surge in trade, which put China's import/export rate ahead of that of some more economically developed countries such as the United Kingdom.

In 2002 China signed an important trade agreement with six other Southeast Asian nations. These countries created the first phase of what will be the world's largest free-trade market, containing 1.7 billion people. Imports of rice and other agricultural produce as well as industrial raw materials such as oil, timber and minerals from this region are increasing.

Containers are lined up neatly, ready for export from Hong Kong.

MAJOR TRADING PARTNERS (% GDP), 2002

EXPORTS

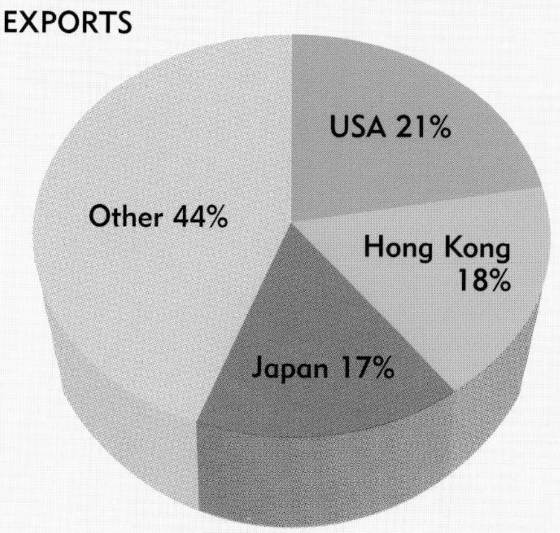

IMPORTS

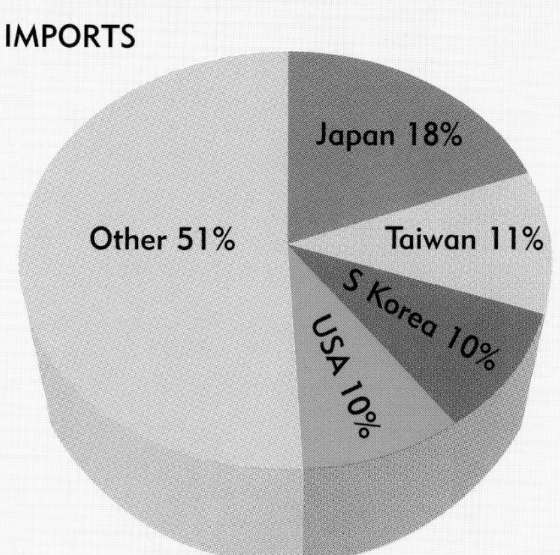

Source: *CIA World Factbook*, 2003

ENVIRONMENTAL CHALLENGES

Sand from the Gobi Desert has almost covered this house in Langtou village, Hebei Province.

Population growth and rapid economic expansion have placed strains on China's environmental resources. Soil erosion, desertification, water scarcity and pollution are just some of the problems China needs to solve to avoid further damage to its environment.

DESERTIFICATION AND SOIL EROSION

Desertification is one of China's major environmental problems, affecting nearly 20 percent of the country. Across northwest China lies a string of deserts, and these are growing at an increasing rate. Desertification is caused in part by low rainfall, and prolonged periods of drought such as the one that happened in 2001 (see page 13) intensify the process. Strong winds also play a major role.

Human activity is a major cause of soil erosion. As good farmland in the eastern regions is absorbed into the growing cities, new areas of land farther west have been cleared for farming use. Forests are cut down to provide land on which to grow grain crops, for example. These activities have exposed the soil to erosion. Wind blows soil away or rain

CASE STUDY
THE LOESS PLATEAU

Heavy rainstorms have cut deep gullies into the loess landscape, which is badly eroded.

The Loess Plateau, part of the Yellow River basin, is the largest area in China affected by soil erosion. Some form of erosion affects nearly three-quarters of the Loess Plateau. The main causes are deforestation in the south and overgrazing in the north. But the loess is also easily eroded by intense summer rainstorms, which cut deep gullies in the steep valley sides.

One of the universities in Shaanxi Province has set up an experimental station to combat soil erosion. Terraces reduce the amount of runoff, allowing the soil to stay in place. Soil is also prevented from being washed away by vegetation planted on the slopes between each terrace. Where the ground is too steep for terraces, trees and grass have been planted.

Water conservation is important, and dry farming (growing crops without the use of irrigation) is practiced. Crops alternate with fallow land so that each summer's rainfall is available for one crop per year. Farmers cover roots in plastic sheeting to stop evaporation.

The Yellow River picks up most of its silt load on its journey through the loess region. As the river crosses the North China Plain, the silt is deposited on the riverbed. This causes the riverbed level to rise, and consequently the river channel cannot carry as much water as before, so it is more likely to flood. Combating soil erosion in the loess region would help reduce the threat of flooding on the North China Plain.

washes it downhill. Another problem is the overstocking of grazing land such that grazing animals clear too much vegetation and expose the soil. Together, desertification and soil erosion result in the loss of 150,000 hectares of farmland each year in Inner Mongolia alone.

Loss of livelihoods for farmers through crop or land damage are major problems. In addition, industry and transport can be adversely affected by dust storms from desert areas, and sandstorms affect a much wider area than dust storms. Ten provinces were affected in 2002.

FINDING SOLUTIONS

Each year, China spends vast sums of money fighting desertification. China's State Forestry Administration has started several major projects aimed at halting desertification and soil erosion, and so have provincial and local governments. In Qinghai some grassland areas are being forested, and in one area of Tibet farmland is being returned to grass and trees. Grazing of livestock has been replaced by dry-lot feeding – keeping the livestock in pens and feeding them with fodder. People are also being encouraged to plant trees to help control the advance of the deserts.

During the severe drought of 2000 people collected fish from puddles in a dried-up lake in Beijing.

WATER SCARCITY

Having enough water is essential for development, since it is needed by people, agriculture and industry. As China's population and economy continue to grow, demands on its water will become greater. But water scarcity is a major problem. It is particularly severe in the North China Plain, where demands for water are greatest. Water resources are most abundant in the southwest, where demand is low.

NORTH CHINA PLAIN

The North China Plain has low rainfall of 400–900mm a year. It is also home to about 300 million to 325 million people – more than a quarter of the country's population. To meet food requirements, the land under irrigation has been doubled. Farmers use large amounts of water from the region's underlying aquifer – 1,000 tonnes of water grows just one tonne of wheat. In the last 30 years the water table has dropped more than 30m.

At the same time, use of water for irrigation in the upper Yellow River has meant that less water reaches the regions farther down the river. From 1990 until 2001 the river failed to reach the sea for 180 days each year, and during this period it was unable to flush out pollutants.

Both rural and urban areas (especially the cities of Beijing and Tianjin) are now short of water. The situation has reached the crisis point. More than a quarter of China's GDP is earned in this region. Without more water, thousands of people will lose their livelihoods and China's economy will suffer.

CASE STUDY
THE SOUTH-NORTH WATER PROJECT (SNWP)

The South-North Water Project (SNWP) is a plan for transferring water from the Yangtze to the Yellow River basin via three routes. The SNWP is to transfer much-needed water from the Yangtze basin to the North China Plain. The Yangtze's flow is 20 times that of the Yellow River, and only 3 percent of this would be taken by the SNWP.

Like the Three Gorges Dam (see page 21), the SNWP is a highly controversial and expensive project. Opponents argue that more efficient use of water could solve the North China Plain's problem. They also point out that raising the dam of the Danjiangkou reservoir on the middle route will flood the homes of 250,000 people, forcing them to leave. Objectors also believe that diverting water from the Yangtze may affect ecosystems in the Yellow River.

Those in favor of the SNWP argue that without the extra water the scheme will bring, it would be impossible to protect the North China Plain's environment. Lack of water would cause wetlands and deltas to continue to shrink, rivers to dry up, water tables to fall farther and pollution levels to rise.

The Grand Canal will carry water for the eastern route of the SNWP. Beijing and Tianjin will receive water from the project by 2007.

POLLUTION

China's economic growth has been accompanied by serious pollution problems of both water and air.

WATER POLLUTION

In the countryside, agricultural runoff containing chemical fertilizer is a major cause of water pollution. But the increase in town and village enterprises, which often dump waste products into nearby rivers, is making the problem worse. In 1994 the Huaihe River was one of China's most polluted rivers: More than 1,500 businesses in the river basin released untreated waste into the river, and untreated sewage added to the pollution problem. The river's condition sparked a campaign to control the discharge of pollutants. Today, many of the small paper mills that were among the main polluters have been closed down, and 55 new sewage plants are planned.

One of the major environmental concerns over the Three Gorges Dam is the water pollution that will result from drowning both urban and rural areas along the sides of the reservoir. On 1 June 2003 the reservoir started to fill. By 2009, 13 cities, 140 towns and 1,300 villages will have been submerged. Pollutants from these places and the surrounding lands will enter the reservoir.

CASE STUDY
SUZHOU CREEK

Before Suzhou Creek was cleaned up, people were driven away by the smell. Now shoppers buy produce from a bridge over the water.

Since 1989 cities have been turning their attention to environmental issues. Suzhou Creek in Shanghai was notoriously polluted. The water was dark-colored and stank of untreated sewage and industrial effluent. Today, though, the water has been cleaned and a green corridor beside the creek is being established – an ideal spot for practicing early morning t'ai chi. The project is scheduled for completion in 2010, by which time the water should be clean enough to support aquatic life.

Smoke from coal-burning stoves such as this one is a major contributor to China's air pollution problem.

Air Pollution

Air pollution is a big problem in China's major cities, where pollution levels are published in the daily papers. Traffic emissions, which are increasing as more people buy cars, are partly responsible. So, too, are industrial pollutants, sulfur dioxide from coal-burning thermal power stations and the coal-dust briquettes burned on household stoves.

Heavy industries are major polluters of China's cities. Shenyang, in the northeast industrial area, was one of the world's ten most-polluted cities. In 2000, emissions of harmful gases and heavy metal from Shenyang's smelting plant were so bad that the plant was forced to close down. In Beijing, Tianjin and other cities on the North China Plain, each spring severe dust storms and sandstorms lasting two to four days add to the misery of residents. The sand is blown in from dunes that are steadily creeping closer to Beijing and are now only 240km away. In March 2000, to strengthen its bid for the 2008 Olympics, Beijing began planting trees to form a windbreak around the city that would offer protection from dust storms. Tianjin followed suit. A belt of trees 4,480km long, called the "Great Green Wall," is to be planted along the southern edge of the Gobi Desert in an attempt to stop its expansion. A sandstorm monitoring system (there are 20 stations so far) can alert cities four days ahead of advancing storms.

ENVIRONMENTAL PROTECTION

Balancing population growth and economic growth against the needs of the environment is extremely difficult for LEDCs. Fifty years of development have taken their toll on China's environment. Today, however, protecting the environment is part of the country's overall plan to develop in a way that will not harm future generations.

A series of important environmental protection measures has already been put into action, including projects aimed at reducing soil erosion. In 1998 a ban on logging in the upper Yangtze region was introduced, and in March 2000 the "Grain for Green" campaign began along the river's upper reaches. Grain for Green pays farmers to return cropland to grass and forest. The program has now also been adopted in the middle Yangtze province of Hunan.

ACID RAIN

Coal burning, which produces 90 percent of China's sulfur dioxide emissions, is a major cause of acid rain. The worst-affected areas are south of the Yangtze, for example Guangdong Province in the Pearl River Delta. The effects of acid rain are also increasingly being felt in eastern coastal areas.

PROTECTING WILDLIFE

One of China's key wildlife-protection projects is saving the giant panda, of which there may only be about 1,000 left in the wild. The pandas live in bamboo forests, and their habitat is under threat from illegal loggers and encroaching farmland. Both fragment the forest, isolating small panda communities.

DESULFURIZATION

The government has taken steps to limit the amount of sulfur dioxide emissions. These include use of clean coal and clean combustion technologies, taxes that punish polluters financially and a ban on building new coal-burning power stations in large cities. Desulfurization technology has to be installed where sulfur emissions exceed 1 percent. Further reductions in pollution levels are required by 2010.

People work on a forest-planting project on the outskirts of Beijing. A ring of trees around the city will reduce the impact of sand storms.

In 1980, the Giant Panda Breeding Research Base was set up in Chengdu. Three years later, the Woolong Nature Reserve, 160km away, was founded. A joint venture between Woolong and the Panda Trust (based in the UK) aims to plant bamboo "corridors" connecting one panda habitat to another, in the hope that pandas will be able to move from place to place along them. If the corridors prove successful, then a whole network will be established. Eventually, buffer zones will be planted either side of the 0.5-km wide green corridors, allowing the pandas to travel with less disturbance.

ENVIRONMENTAL EDUCATION

Study of the environment forms part of China's national curriculum at primary and middle levels. Good coverage in the press is promoting wider awareness of environmental issues. Activities such as National Tree Planting Day are practical ways in which everyone in China can make a positive contribution to protecting the country's environment.

CASE STUDY
TOURISM AND THE YUNNAN GREAT RIVERS REGION

The Yunnan Great Rivers area is about the size of West Virginia. Visitors are attracted by the region's fantastic mountain scenery and its biodiversity (variety of plants and animals). Yunnan Great Rivers is one of the world's most important biodiversity sites. The region is also home to Naxi and Tibetans, both ethnic minorities in China.

To conserve the region's landscapes, biodiversity and cultures, the Yunnan government also sought and gained World Natural Heritage listing. The lake areas – Napa and Bita – are among the 15 named areas. Napa Lake is surrounded by wetland and meadows that are covered in flowers from spring through autumn. Increasing numbers of visitors have started to come to the region. The goal is to expand tourism without compromising the environment.

The Woolong Nature Reserve has the largest number of wild pandas in the world.

Acid rain Rainfall that is more acid than usual because it contains dissolved pollutants such as sulfur dioxide and nitrous oxides.

Aftershock Earth tremors that occur after the main earthquake.

Agribusiness Commercial farming on a large scale. It is highly mechanized and dependent on chemicals, and it is often owned by finance companies.

Aquifer A layer of porous rock that stores water.

Arable land Land that is suitable for growing crops.

Arid climate A term describing a climate with too little moisture to sustain farming.

Biodiversity The variety of species found within an area.

Delta A triangular-shaped landscape feature made up of sediments transported by a river and deposited at its mouth.

Desertification Creation of desertlike conditions in arid areas, usually by human activities, such as overgrazing and deforestation.

Dry farming Growing crops in areas of low rainfall but without the use of irrigation.

Earthquake The rapid movement of rocks in the Earth's crust, causing shock waves.

Economic development The process of economic change that leads to higher standards of living.

Ecosystem The contents of an environment, including all the plants and animals that live in it.

Epicenter The point on the Earth's surface vertically above the origin of an earthquake.

Floodplain The wide floor of a river valley over which it may flood.

GDP (Gross Domestic Product) The monetary value of goods and services produced by a country in a single year.

GNI (Gross National Income) The monetary value of goods and services produced by a country plus any earnings from overseas in a single year. It used to be known as Gross National Product (GNP).

Hydroelectric power (HEP) Electricity generated by using the power of water.

Immigrant A person who comes to live in a new country.

Infrastructure The basic economic foundations of a country, such as roads, bridges, communication networks and sewerage systems.

Intensive farming Maximizing the use of the land by growing more than one crop on the same piece of land at the same time.

Irrigation Watering the land by using channels, drip systems or sprinkler systems.

Karst landscape Limestone uplands into which erosion has carved surface crevices and underground caves and streams.

Less Economically Developed Country (LEDC) A country with poor living standards and usually limited manufacturing industries.

Levee A raised bank that is formed naturally by a river, although people may build them up higher as a form of flood protection.

Loess Fine, powdery clay and silt carried by strong winds from Central Asia.

Migration The movement of people from one living area to another.

Monsoon climate A weather system that has a seasonal reversal of pressure and wind direction over land masses and neighboring seas.

Permafrost Permanently frozen subsoil.

Plateau An area of fairly level high ground.

Richter scale A measurement used to determine the size and intensity of an earthquake.

Runoff The overland movement of water after rainfall.

Soil erosion The wearing away and transportation of the soil layer.

Tectonic plates Large areas of the Earth's crust floating on top of its molten core.

Transnational company (TNC) A large company with factories in several countries that trades globally.

Tributary A stream or river that flows into a larger river.

Typhoon A violent tropical storm originating at sea.

Urbanization The development and growth of an urban (city) area.

Water table The upper level of water in an aquifer.

BOOKS TO READ:

Cotterell, Arthur. *Eyewitness Guides: Ancient China*. New York: Dorling Kindersley, 2000. A colorfully illustrated guide to China's history and culture for ages 8 to 12.

Dutemple, Lesley. *The Great Wall of China*. Minneapolis, Minnesota: Lerner Publications Company, 2002. An illustrated history of this centuries-long construction project for ages 12 and up.

Harper, Damian. *National Geographic Traveler: China*. Washington, D.C.: National Geographic, 2001. Informative travel guide for all ages.

Keeler, Stephen. *The Changing Face of China*. Milwaukee, Wisconsin: Raintree Publishers, 2002. Illustrated reference for ages 9 and up.

Winchester, Simon. *The River at the Center of the World*. New York: Henry Holt, 1997. A travel narrative mainly about the Yangtze but with plenty of general information about life in present-day China.

WEBSITES:

CHINATOWN
Useful information about Chinese culture:
www.chinatown-online.com

GENERAL INFORMATION:
Online version of China's English-language newspaper:
www.chinadaily.com.cn

DUST STORMS AND DESERTIFICATION:
www.gluckman.com/ChinaDesert.html

POPULATION:
www.prcdc.org/summaries/china/china.html

USEFUL ADDRESSES:

China National Tourist Office
600 W. Broadway, Suite 320
Glendale, CA 91204

Chinese Embassy (Education Section)
2300 Connecticut Avenue N.W.
Washington, D.C. 20008

METRIC CONVERSION TABLE

To convert	to	do this
mm (millimeters)	inches	divide by 25.4
cm (centimeters)	inches	divide by 2.54
m (meters)	feet	multiply by 3.281
m (meters)	yards	multiply by 1.094
km (kilometers)	yards	multiply by 1094
km (kilometers)	miles	divide by 1.6093
kilometers per hour	miles per hour	divide by 1.6093
cm^2 (square centimeters)	square inches	divide by 6.452
m^2 (square meters)	square feet	multiply by 10.76
m^2 (square meters)	square yards	multiply by 1.196
km^2 (square kilometers)	square miles	divide by 2.59
km^2 (square kilometers)	acres	multiply by 247.1
hectares	acres	multiply by 2.471
cm^3 (cubic centimeters)	cubic inches	multiply by 16.387
m^3 (cubic meters)	cubic yards	multiply by 1.308
l (liters)	pints	multiply by 2.113
l (liters)	gallons	divide by 3.785
g (grams)	ounces	divide by 28.329
kg (kilograms)	pounds	multiply by 2.205
metric tonnes	short tons	multiply by 1.1023
metric tonnes	long tons	multiply by 0.9842
BTUs (British thermal units)	kWh (kilowatt-hours)	divide by 3,415.3
watts	horsepower	multiply by 0.001341
kWh (kilowatt-hours)	horsepower-hours	multiply by 1.341
MW (megawatts)	horsepower	multiply by 1,341
gigawatts per hour	horsepower per hour	multiply by 1,341,000
°C (degrees Celsius)	°F (degrees Fahrenheit)	multiply by 1.8 then add 32

Skyscrapers dominate the view of Hong Kong's central business district.

Golden lions guard the entrance to the Forbidden City, Beijing.

Karst hills form a stunning backdrop in Guilin.